THE LIFE
THE HEART SPROUTS

*"Keep thy heart with all diligence;
for out of it are the issues of life."*

Also by Torry Fountinhead

The 7 Pillars Your Authentic Self Stands On, Part I of *The Essential Companion Series*

The Beauty, Part I of *The Contemplation Series*

The Soul's Oppener – Enchanting The Soul to 'Being'

Part II of *The Contemplation Series*

Shush! It's a Secret, The Lake Hides His Dummy, Part of *The Rainbow of Life's Secrets*

Poem: Good Enough, Part of *Forever Spoken, The International Library of Poetry*

A Tip of an Iceberg Meditations, a series of short books (see the series' list at http://atipofanicebergmeditations.ca)

and many more at work…

THE LIFE
THE HEART SPROUTS

*"Keep thy heart with all diligence;
for out of it are the issues of life."*

Part III of "A Tip of an Iceberg Meditations"
Series

By

Torry Fountinhead

Airé Libré Publishing & Computing Ltd.

eBook ISBNs:
ISBN-10: 0-9781499-7-1
ISBN-13: 978-0-9781499-7-0
Print Book ISBNs:
ISBN-10: 0-9781498-0-7
ISBN-13: 978-0-9781498-0-2

Etz Chaim designed by D&D, Lake George NY USA

© 2017 Torry Fountinhead
All Rights of this work are Reserved. No part or whole may be used, copied or reproduced, stored in retrieval systems, or transmitted, in any form or by any means whatsoever, including electronic media, mechanical, photocopying, recording, or otherwise.

For more information contact:
Airé Libré Publishing & Computing Ltd.
Suite 306, 185-911 Yates St.
Victoria BC V8V 4Y9 Canada
Tel: 1-250-592-3099.
http://www.al.bc.ca   info@al.bc.ca

Book Web-Site URLs:
http://thelifetheheartsprouts.atipofanicebergmeditations.ca

Part of:
Http://www.atipofanicebergmeditations.ca
Http://www.tipofaniceberg.ca
Http://www.atipofanicebergmeditations.com
Http://www.tipofaniceberg.com

Key Points:

- The Life The Heart Sprouts i
- The Life The Heart Sprouts iii
- Key Points: v
- The Life The Heart Sprouts vii
  - Prologue 1
  - Within the core of your being 5
  - The treasure within 8
  - Focus 11
  - Dedication 14
  - Steadfastness 17
  - Righteousness 21
  - Guarding oneself 24
  - Health 28
  - Results 32
  - Speech 36
  - Choosing your path 43
  - Choosing the Right 47
  - Wisdom of the ages 50
  - A word about this series 55
  - Notes 57

vi

THE LIFE
THE HEART SPROUTS

*"Keep thy heart with all diligence;
for out of it are the issues of life."*

Prologue

In a previous book, I shared with you my idiom:

How hidden, yet revealed daily, is the wisdom of the ages.

Here, I am bringing to you a quote from the book of Proverbs, part of the Bible's Old Testament, and hope you will find how astonishing it is in its accuracy.

It seems, as if, Human nature did not change in essence since our creation, and certainly not since Solomon the king wrote Proverbs.

The anatomy and connection between our heart, minds, and soul, inclusive of our behaviour and habits, is essentially working in the same way, even if our surroundings and conditions of life are different. Therefore, we could benefit from this wisdom of old.

I also bring you the actual quote from Proverbs in its original in Hebrew, and two English translations.

Proverbs 4/20-27 from King James Version (KJV)

4:20 My son, attend to my words; incline thine ear unto my sayings.

4:21 Let them not depart from thine eyes; keep them in the midst of thine heart.

4:22 For they are life unto those that find them, and health to all their flesh.

4:23 Keep thy heart with all diligence; for out of it [are] the issues of life.

4:24 Put away from thee a froward mouth, and perverse lips put far from thee.

4:25 Let thine eyes look right on, and let thine eyelids look straight before thee.

4:26 Ponder the path of thy feet, and let all thy ways be established.

4:27 Turn not to the right hand nor to the left: remove thy foot from evil.

Proverbs 4/20-27 from English Standard Version (ESV)

20 My son, be attentive to my words; incline your ear to my sayings.

21 Let them not escape from your sight; keep them within your heart.

22 For they are life to those who find them, and healing to all their flesh.

23 Keep your heart with all vigilance, for from it flow the springs of life.

24 Put away from you crooked speech, and put devious talk far from you.

25 Let your eyes look directly forward, and your gaze be straight before you.

26 Ponder the path of your feet; then all your ways will be sure.

27 Do not swerve to the right or to the left; turn your foot away from evil.

Proverbs 4/20-27 from the original Hebrew

כ) בְּנִי לִדְבָרַי הַקְשִׁיבָה לַאֲמָרַי הַט אָזְנֶךָ

כא) אַל-יַלִּיזוּ מֵעֵינֶיךָ שָׁמְרֵם בְּתוֹךְ לְבָבֶךָ

כב) כִּי-חַיִּים הֵם לְמֹצְאֵיהֶם וּלְכָל-בְּשָׂרוֹ מַרְפֵּא

כג) מִכָּל-מִשְׁמָר נְצֹר לִבֶּךָ כִּי-מִמֶּנּוּ תּוֹצְאוֹת חַיִּים

כד) הָסֵר מִמְּךָ עִקְּשׁוּת פֶּה וּלְזוּת שְׂפָתַיִם הַרְחֵק מִמֶּךָ

כה) עֵינֶיךָ לְנֹכַח יַבִּיטוּ וְעַפְעַפֶּיךָ יַיְשִׁרוּ נֶגְדֶּךָ

כו) פַּלֵּס מַעְגַּל רַגְלֶךָ וְכָל-דְּרָכֶיךָ יִכֹּנוּ

כז) אַל-תֵּט יָמִין וּשְׂמֹאול הָסֵר רַגְלְךָ מֵרָע

Within the core of your being

In your heart of hearts, in the core of your being, where all is sacred and holy – and good, exists the Light and vitality of your Life.

That which makes you alive – that which makes you, You.

This force within you is the one that facilitate the life you live, the quality, and the story.

Your life story, in all its shades and complications alas, is not only dependent on this part of you, but include the more immediate part of your daily conscious, and mind.

Your capabilities, and everything else about you, are a derivative of the whole of you, as there is a sort of a handshake between your conscious mind, and that, which is within you.

I refrain from calling the inner part, your sub-conscious, as to my mind there is much more involved.

You see, each and every cell of your body has its own consciousness. Your body also has a myriad of beings, both beneficial, and some others that are not so beneficial, each with its own ability to influence the whole.

Your outer life influences your immediate mind and consciousness. It creates ripples within you that produce all colours of thoughts and feelings. Those, in turn, awaken some similar thoughts and feelings from your past, and amplify them to a degree.

Habits rise, for good or bad, behaviour demonstrated, whether wanted or unwanted, gentle or hurtful, and where are You at that time?

At this time, it is important that you will understand that you are not a singular homogeneous unit, with one singular response.

You are a multi-being, not only by the multitude of your parts, but also the actual beings that comprise you.

Please be not alarmed, as all Human Beings are exactly the same in this regard, and if it were not for it being so, we would not exist at all.

With your understanding, I hope you will gain the importance of 'directing' yourself in such a way that you may act in life more like a steady arrow, than flaky seeds blown by the wind.

Your inner part is the one that holds the hands on the rudder of your boat – allows it to have then the Right direction, and it will paint your outer picture, as you really wish it to be.

One may also imagine a powerful force gathering all the strings to one bunch, which then may become a solid and strong rope to be used in the varied tasks of life.

Let us then understand that the inner force is the one that may give us the life we live and thus, we must inform it unilaterally in an enlightened way, so the message will be One and thus, clear.

The treasure within

The treasure within you is that golden nugget, that unpolished diamond that gives you your uniqueness.

This is most important to comprehend – you ARE unique. The Creator is not a Human manufacturing plant owner that has an assembly line of identical robot-like beings!

I prefer to use the analogy of a prism, which describes each person as a prism that shines the Divine Light in their own personal, and individual way – not two are alike.

Your inner life force and consciousness is the one that brings forth the connection to the Whole Creation and thus, inspires you to shine the light in your own special way – assuming you are actually listening.

This inner golden nugget cannot be spoiled. It might not be displayed, or used, but it will remain there forever, as it is part of your eternal self – whether you believe it or not.

Human Beings always knew that, at their core, there is a special strength, a force, which no one could destroy, this is why most Humans always rise to the challenge, or keep hopeful outlook, or try to evolve under any, and all conditions.

Imagine this part of you as an ever-flowing fountainhead, which springs forth continuously, so you may drink the waters of Life, and live.

Your sub-conscious, which is the facilitator of your life's creation, uses this force directly, endlessly creating that which you aspire to, thoughtfully, or not, willingly, or not.

You may gather how important it is to be inspired by this inner unspoiled part of you.

Furthermore, 'drinking' from this inner source, versus from other sources, is like drinking pure water versus mucky ones.

Therefore, your whole self has to live every day in such a manner that will have direct contact with this inner treasure of yours, *neglecting to do so, results in wasting time and effort.*

Focus

One solid and indisputable truth is that 'Life is work.'

What do I mean by work?

We are constantly evolving, growing, developing, moving etc. within an ever-changing life whereby, anything from the environment down to thoughts are constantly changing and moving.

In order to move in a straight line versus zigzagging, and maybe 'getting lost in the woods', we have to understand how to navigate the constant changing of Life.

Focus is the tool to use to bring forth a dedicated movement.

Even in a dance that forms an artwork displayed for the enjoyment of others, there would be a choreographer, which will compose a set of movements, as per the theme of the dance, and the message it tries to convey.

The difference between hearing and listening, as another mode of input, is the one that illustrates how a person may be able to internalise a message, or idea. This is why Solomon the king started his message of Proverbs, quoted in the beginning of this book [Proverbs 4/20], with "... be attentive to my words, incline your ear to my sayings."

When you listen attentively, your whole being is engaged, every fibre of your being is called to attention, and then you receive the full value of what actually was said.

Solomon the king continues to say [Proverbs 4/21] "Let them not escape from your sight;

keep them within your heart."

Solomon the king also used more than one of our senses to illustrate how we may be engaged fully.

Do you see the importance conveyed herein?

In order to keep something at your sight – you would not be able to pay attention to 'lesser' things, nor would you be able to stray away from your target.

To keep something within your heart will entrust your inner self with guarding it diligently, constantly, and faithfully.

Therefore, focusing in life may grant you the ability to have a solid foundation to your movement, and growth. A steadier advance will be your constant gift.

One may be tempted to list all that the opposite may cause in one's life, but let us, at this stage, concentrate on the positive that creates a forward movement, and forsake the negative that might stall us, or even cause us to be moving with hardship.

Dedication

To what are we dedicated to in life?

To what should we be dedicated to in life?

May we be dedicated to more than one thing in life?

Dedication is a serious matter. It is a promise, something that may be cast in stone. Therefore, we should be serious when committing ourselves, as much as we should be careful as to what.

When we are set on a course of action, many a times we might be swept by it, so much so that we would not notice if and when we might bring harm, either to ourselves, or others.

A very simple example of dedication would be a dedication of a book by its author that once printed, may not be taken back.

A more serious example would be a memorial dedication that the namesake might prove to be unworthy.

Even more serious than that would be when we dedicate ourselves to another person, or cause, only to discover that we may have been taken advantage of, and meanwhile, lost time, resources, and peace of mind thus, jeopardising our health, and even our reputation, not to mention being off our own path.

What, therefore, constitutes a 'just' dedication?

If you check with the Oxford dictionary, you would find that the first meaning of 'dedicate' is akin to 'devote' – this is a very special meaning, as in order to devote oneself to a cause, person, or goal, one has to do it wholly – with a whole heart, and maybe even heart, mind, and soul.

This might be the reason why Solomon the King used not less than eight verses to describe what his message entails.

Solomon the King asks you to listen, be attentive, mindful, caring, and faithful. He gives you behavioural methods to follow, so there would be no chance of you losing your way, and the seriousness of the matter.

Life is not a whim-full thing whereby, you can jump from here to there aimlessly. Surely you are familiar with the premise that the 'shortest distance between two points is a straight line'?

Steadfastness

Steadfastness is the mark of a consistent, firm, and unwavering behaviour – like a well-balanced arrow on its 'direct' way to the aimed.

In verses 24 through 27 [Proverbs 4], Solomon the King gives specific instruction on how to create this 'direct' manner of proceeding.

Let us first ask the question why steadfastness is required.

Human Beings are different from other creatures in that that we have a thinking mind, which can take over our best interest and highest good.

Animals, mostly, follow that which is for their highest chance for survival, as otherwise, they are benefiting from nature without reservation, or judgement.

Only those animals that are in close relationship with Humans exhibit emotional disturbances resulting from those relationships.

Humans have another peculiar trait, they want to ascend nature, but at the same time are obsessed with the physical – they want to live in Spirit, but judge everything as it relates to their body and possessions. They also use nature to their own benefit, regardless of the damage it inflicts on them, and the whole of Earth.

You may ask, how can steadfastness benefit us in such a state of affairs?

Let us go back a step, and remind ourselves of our uniqueness, value, preciousness, and importance. We are here for a reason.

If each person will remember their own importance, they would also remember the other persons' importance.

Like planets in orbit, we may share a solar system, a galaxy, or the whole universe, but we do not have to collide, or even destroy, in order to live well.

I can hear you saying, oh! what about the colliding of asteroids?

Well, in Life there are many unknown reasons, despite our scientists trying to explain them, and yet, the planets are still orbiting on, and on.

In similar way that each plant is dedicated to its orbit, and stage of life, so are we in the swarm that is Humanity.

Therefore, remember your uniqueness. Remember that even if you are not sure of your life's purpose, vocation, or aim, you are still entitled to 'orbit' in life, as per your abilities.

Set your heart in a devotional manner to live your life in a way that follows your highest good, and the highest good of all.

Try not to waste neither your time, effort, attention, thought, nor energy, and step forward in a loving manner, like an arrow on its way to the aimed. Arguments, battles, wars, competition, and strife, are not a 'must' in Life – flow is the natural state.

When you read the key point about Health, and consult verse 23, you would understand the implications of not being steadfastly dedicated.

Righteousness

Righteousness, unfortunately, may be somewhat of a misunderstood word, as the righteous people are considered very few, and the self-righteous are considered the many.

In reality, the word's source is 'Right', which brings us back to ask what is Right?

Throughout the centuries, Human Beings

proved themselves to be creatures enslaved by their own opinion and thus, became judgemental, unforgiving, and even hostile.

Creation is one. We do not know what was there before, who had created creation, or how did it start. Forgive me scientists, but I think that we are all still at a level of a kindergarten regarding the understanding of how creation became.

Many billions of people on Earth tend to believe in the One Creator, the One, God, or any name you would call that singular presence that we would like to have faith in, and grant characteristics that might help us to live life in a happier manner.

We have books of wisdom, of which the Bible is one, listing for us pearls of wisdom designated to lead us to a life of lesser strife.

Yet, inwardly, we have an innate knowing of the existence of Right and Wrong.

Imagine then how would it be if we would stop the chaos created by our anxieties, opinions, reactions, and actions, and turn inwardly to explore what is the Right response for any given circumstance.

One must ask if love, respect, and appreciation would have been the chosen frame of mind, if our world would not have been a better place to live in.

Guarding oneself

In verse 23 [Proverbs 4], Solomon the King brings the important aspect of the heart.

Guarding oneself is guarding your existence, your actual being.

Guarding your heart is what will facilitate it.

The Life The Heart Sprouts

Solomon the King says: "Keep thy heart with all diligence..." guard it as you never guard anything else – do not fail!

Actually, there is another verse, which the old sages coined, based on this wisdom, and it says, "If I am not there for myself, who would be there for me" [Avot 1/14]. Of course, I am simplifying here, but you get the idea – we, the adults and able, are each responsible for ourselves, we must take care, and guard that which promise our existence, but not by sacrificing another, or even harming them.

Solomon the King just highlights for us the fact that our heart (on all its levels) is the organ of creation – the fountainhead of what will be. Our heart affects all the levels of our being, physical, emotional, intellectual, and all other.

How many times we hear about people's 'broken heart', or 'heart attack', or 'elated heart'.

Pandora's box had only one good thing in it – Hope. What is hope if not a feeling in our heart that a better time, and or situation, might still be possible?

At war times, it had been observed that once the captured people lost their hope, they died.

A word of caution though, guarding your heart does not mean close your heart; actually, it is quite the opposite. If you keep an open heart and put in it the powers of love, respect, and appreciation, they will be the best guards to stand guard for you.

Society will flourish, as creativity and equanimity flow freely from open hearts – laughter and joy will be present, and will elevate all people, even if they are in the midst of some form of suffering.

How many times we say that in hindsight, we can see all clearly.

What Solomon the King is trying to do is forewarn us, and guide us to lead a life free of our own creation of strife.

This is a very important point.

The strife in our lives may be created by many sources, but we do have some control – we may control ourselves, and our own actions.

Free will is coming here to play a pivotal role. The choices that we make will determine the amount of strife we contribute to our own lives.

Do you need strife?

Do you need to harm yourself?

Do you need to be distracted from your aim in life, just because you did not take into consideration that which may throw you off your path?

Do you need confusion or clarity in your life?

Slow down, contemplate, make a wise choice, proceed with diligence, love thy neighbour as you love yourself – be kind.

Health

At this stage, I would like to go back to Solomon the king verse regarding health [Proverbs 4/22].

The whole message's benefit, within the eight verses, is funnily enough mentioned immediately after the required mode of listening instructions, and just before a warning.

The Life The Heart Sprouts

This is an interesting order in itself.

First, give the benefit, and then, warn for not following the instructions given after. It seems to me that a parental method was employed here to denote a tender loving care for the listener. Almost pleading although, coming from an authoritative figure.

'Life' is promised to those who find the way to actually be aware of their existence, and then listen to them. Furthermore, it promises healing to all our bodily ills, for the whole body.

Solomon the king speaks rather assuredly at the fact that there is a possibility of life and a whole-bodily healing, without any reservations, provided, one adheres to that, which is written in the next verse.

Proverbs verse 4/23 spell out unequivocally that our heart is the fountainhead, of which our lives flow from, and create (issues) that which we experience in life. The word 'issues' may also be referred to as 'results' therefore, as we know, actions bear results – what actions actually brought forth an 'ill' results in our lives?

Here Solomon the king symbolises that our heart/centre, that which is within us, that which is subjective, is influenced directly from our outer being, and how our inner being is affected by it.

It is the force at the core of our being, which facilitate what manifests in our conscious outer life. It is not necessarily a reference to our physical heart, but actually to our proverbial heart.

Here, again, we need to acknowledge the value that our inner self holds, which will override our outer self, in every instance.

If one is truthful in definition, one has only to acknowledge the amount of illnesses, sicknesses, traumas, abuse injuries, and more that exist in the world – it almost seems that there is more suffering than Life.

Yet, Life continue, Life persist on, because growth is natural, sickness only denotes imbalance.

Is it not interesting that all lines of medicine, whether traditional or modern, denote that stress and aggravation, as well as unintended stress, are a direct cause to many of the known illnesses.

We are called to take responsibility over ourselves – the whole of ourselves, not only part of us – to apply preventive medicine, and not only corrective medicine. In actuality, we are promised that if we follow Solomon the king's advice, in any case we will be granted full healing.

    Think first, than act.

Results

The term "issues of life", as was said previously, speaks of the results stemming from the heart condition.

In ancient times, as in this day and age, Human Beings were very much aware of that that actions had consequences, similar to cause and effect.

Even in Quantum Physics, it is spoken of that the results of an experiment will directly be affected by the observer, and or the one who sets up the experiment.

I like the term 'reverse engineering' in so much that it is more readily understood then looking ahead to an unforeseen future result.

In reverse engineering, you would look at an expected result, and judge for yourself whether you like it, or not. Based on your 'liking', you may explore what steps might have brought that result to being, and either take those steps (when you like it), or eliminate them (when you do not).

Wisdom is gained by experiences in life while, knowledge may be learnt. Other people's knowledge might apply to you, and it might not, but your own experience may never falter. Knowledge that you have learnt yourself, during your experiences, may be combined with the actual experience, and form a new pearl of wisdom.

Those pearls of wisdom can be lifesavers when one may start using them more for foresight versus reverse engineering and thus, you hone your skill of seeing a situation from both directions – the beginning, and the result.

You know your heart best. I am not saying that some wise people will not be able to look to your heart, and know it, but you are the only one privy to all its shades.

You may not be aware of all that is in your heart, as what it reveals to you, in every moment, is all that you may bear. Your heart, too, is created with an aim in mind – the aim to guard your existence; this is why it is so sensitive.

If you will look back to some of your experiences, and apply reverse engineering to them, you may find the condition your heart had to be in, in order to produce such results. You may decipher some patterns, and may even find a common cause. Any cause, or causes, can then be lovingly handled by you – to bring forth healing, and resolution.

Think of a tree, even if it has the best environment, it still has to have all of its own parts working harmoniously, in order to bear fruit of a good quality. This fruit also ensures the future of this tree.

Do not underestimate the importance of results, as they can be your greatest hinders, and stop you from going forward, and succeeding in life.

The risk takers may be divided to two camps, the rush, and the courageous. The rush will go forward disregarding warnings, inner or outer. While, the courageous, will go forward knowing their own strength and the importance of their goal, and proceed focused, but with caution, and without sacrificing themselves, or other.

Results may be your teachers, but it is far more pleasant, and wise, to let your heart be your main teacher.

Your heart will never mislead you, while, your vanity, or ego, might.

Speech

Solomon the king instructs us, very purposefully, regarding speech.

If you may imagine speech to be like the wind, you would see that you are both a vessel of reception, and of send-off.

You breathe-in the life force vitality, and you breathe-out the remainder of what is left of this life force imbued with your own energies, as well as a change in composition.

Your words ride on these breathes, so if you are emotionally affected, the type of energies in respect to those emotions will be spouting from you – gently, or not. For the same token, it also depends where you are, as to what quality of breathe you take in.

While in nature, all on your own, where the air is rich and pure – the life force vitality is pure and strong. While, in the company of others, and or in unnatural places, the life force that surrounds you will carry others' energies on it, including those of the environment.

The connection between our thoughts and emotions effects our expression on every level, and mostly with our speech unless, we restrain ourselves in mature effort to 'choose' a more positive expression.

This restrain, I am referring to, is the basis of a great power, because it allows you to act with your highest good in mind, as well as the highest good of all, which means that you will not delay feeling good, or having any good reach you.

In the old days, people used to say 'vanity,

vanity...', these days they are mentioning the ego. I would rather call a spade a spade, and say that when you are being told something that hurts you or insults you – your prime concern *should* be, to find out from within yourself, why you actually feel hurt, or insulted.

The last thing you should do is to lash back at your seeming assailant. If you answer them back, you give them power, and the knowledge that you have a weak point that they may use in the future – as they please!

On the other hand, if you acknowledge within yourself what is it that needs attending to, attempt to heal this part of you, and respond from a place of calmness and surety, no one will have their power over you.

Speech is very close to the state of our thoughts therefore, I would like to use another biblical story as an analogy, to demonstrate how self-control may be achieved.

Surely, you have heard about Noah's ark story from the Bible [Genesis chapters 5-9]. Well, my analogy goes as follows:

The ark here symbolises the mind, and the animal symbolise our thoughts.

The variety of the animals that were brought into the ark denote the variety of thoughts expressed in our mind (whether we initiate them, or they are initiated by others) whereas, the fact that the animals were brought male and female denotes that the thoughts should be 'balanced', like yin and yang versus, one-sided / unbalanced which may only cause turmoil.

Noah's name originates in the Hebrew language, and actually means 'comfortable', or 'rested'. Being comfortable and rested does mean being at peace within oneself.

Let us use Noah as a person that symbolises you.

Your ark therefore, is your mind, and your own responsibility, which, as the story goes, is the means to your survival.

In addition, in the story, God instructed Noah to build the ark, and we may take it as the inspiration of your Higher Self to help you with your own survival.

Your first responsibility is to manage the thoughts that enter your mind, and how you relate to them. The thoughts should be 'natural and balanced', and be given only the necessary feed, and not more.

Further on, Noah also brought in his immediate family, which we may acquaint to your dearly beloved, both people and aspirations.

When the flood came, the ark rose with the waters, and remained safe and sealed.

Our consciousness is often symbolised, and akin to water, and while our mind (ark) is intact and monitored, our consciousness may now show us its content, and engulf us with its knowing, drowning any harmful influence, as we concentrate solely onto it.

Forty days and forty nights was the period of seclusion that all were in the ark, and it shows the need to take time off for the Self. Only in set period of seclusion, without any influence from the outside, can we really look within.

We may learn a vast amount of the truth about ourselves, if we only look within, provided, we look within lovingly, and not with the others' critical methods, and opinions. I did mention in the first key point that we are good at our core, and we must remember it specifically, in the face of opposition.

The dove in the story symbolises a pure

peaceful thought that is sent out from within ourselves to 'test the waters'. The fact that in the story the dove had returned at first, as it had no place to land, denotes that we, too, have to test our surroundings, and whether we may communicate with others positively, and if not, return to our own seclusion for another short time.

When at last, in the story, the dove returned, and with an olive leaf in its mouth, it indicated that life is found – where there is life, there are positive promoting thoughts, and there is a chance for growth.

The olive leaf is yet another symbol, as the olive tree is a blessed one, from which we have olive oil that was used both for light and for nourishment, and in the Bible olive oil symbolises joy as well. It was an olive leaf, and not any other, that was brought back.

The knowledge that one may find affirmativeness out there is to grant us relief, but with no rush. Noah did stay for further seven days in the ark before attempting to remove the covering of the ark, and make sure that it is safe to step out onto a dry land.

It is always important to test the ground before one is stepping forward, and so it is with a verbal self-expression.

Coming to the end of my long analogy, you may discern how important it is to guard oneself in a way that is quiet, gentle, loving, and productive.

The key is to remember that any speech that comes from 'reactiveness' will land you in a deeper trouble while, taking time-off, managing yourself (thoughts ,emotions, and all) will prove to be more beneficial to you. Therefore, when Solomon the king says: *"Put away from thee a froward mouth, and perverse lips put far from thee."* [Proverbs 4/24], he actually advises you to think first, and choose your words carefully, in addition to refraining from uttering harmful and entangling words.

I brought Noah's story, as an analogy, to make it easier to remember the importance of how to control our minds and actions – to associate it with an helping imaginary.

Choosing your path

I love Solomon the King words in verse 26 [Proverb 4], "Ponder the path of thy feet, and let thy ways be established."

If one looks at the original wording of the verse in Hebrew, in addition to the above English understanding, an image comes to mind, as follows:

Use a level to straighten out the circular movement of your legs. Thus, all your ways (roads) will be direct.

Of course, a meandering path, or a winding path, might sound more interesting – even romantic, but in life it might ask too much of us.

The idea of your life-path should differ from any path we happen to be walking on in our physical experience.

For example, if one would like to choose a life-path of a composer, surely, you would not ask them to spend their life working the land from morning to night.

If one likes to be a shepherd, surely, you will not find them racing cars.

A life-path is a term used mostly to denote the major theme one's life is to take, and thus informs all their choices, and actions.

Our forefathers went very far in trying to understand it, and even invented some tools to know more about it, like Astrology, Numerology, and more.

In ancient medicine, you may also find elements, and constitutions that will try to explain how to treat people in different ways.

We are coming back to the idea that we are all unique, and so is the variation of our life-paths.

Yet, the extent of our meandering is depended on our ability to focus, and dedicate ourselves while, proceeding in life towards our own goal, fulfilling our own vocation, or purpose.

Have you read the children's story of the race that the rabbit and tortoise have entered?

Here we have the perception of speed (rabbit) versus the dedication of purpose (tortoise). It is not the speed that matters, if one is solely relying on it, and neglects to stay on the path; it is the ability to proceed with steadfastness that will determine if you will fulfill your mission.

How about envisaging yourself as an idea in the mind of The Creator, this idea has a mission, vocation, and purpose, and is given gifts, talents, and abilities to achieve them.

You, the idea, is born and has to go through preparation period whereby, learning, experience, and knowledge are to be gained, as means of readiness.

You are set free to choose the best way to go

about fulfilling the idea, and your life-path is the safest and shortest route for you to do so.

Alas, you are born as a Human Being, and therefore, influenced by many things, as well as by your desires, fancies, wants, and fears. Here it is where your life-path and the path you take in your life might differ.

The outside influence may come in the form of demands over you, or even teachers, some of which will tell you that you choose your purpose – it is not written, and others that may tell you that to reach a state of peace and joy in your heart – you have to follow your heart.

You are still to find out who, or what, informed your heart, and what is Right for you.

Choosing the Right

Solomon the King verse 27 [Proverbs 4] is the one that sheds light upon how to choose the Right.

Although the English translation states: "Turn not to the right hand nor to the left; remove thy foot from evil", the Hebrew original tries again to speak in symbolic ideas.

Do not turn right or left – means in actuality walk straight. Although, the Hebrew word 'turn' might be understood as 'lean', so in essence we have a repetition here of the idea of 'be righteous' in all your proceedings. Do not swerve toward any wrong doings, justified, or not.

The choice of word of 'leg' (in Hebrew it says leg versus foot) – remove it from evil, already speaks volumes at the fact that there is such a thing as wrongdoing. That our actions are the ones we should look at, and not only our thoughts, as our legs are moved by our actions, which are moved by our intentions – 'you walk the talk'.

It is an important fact that Solomon the King written these words, because one has to take into consideration what he believed to be right and wrong. Solomon the King was educated based on the Torah and the Ten Commandments, which specify in a detailed manner how should people behave, among themselves, and in relation to God.

There would be no doubt, as to what he will consider Right or Wrong, Good or Evil.

Today, regardless of religion, philosophies, and or ethics, we still feel that, among men, crime appears in 'Wrong' column, and charity in the 'Right' column, and among nations, collaboration appears in the 'Right' column while, war appears in the 'Wrong' one.

It comes back to what we know innately in our heart of hearts.

Our hearts do not lie to us!

Wisdom of the ages

One should take into consideration those writing methods that affected the writing habit in ancient times.

Writing was done on tablets, skins parchment, papyrus, rice paper, and linen, all of which were lengthy in producing, and costly to afford.

Therefore, writing was minimal, and concentrated on what the writers deemed important. Unlike today's vast writing that spans any subject that Humans can imagine.

The writers, therefore, thought of what was important to pass along in their societies, for education, as much as for posterity.

Looking at ancient writings, we can find that many times the writers weaved pearls of wisdom in the midst of historical stories. This even makes it more fascinating when the writing was done for education only – like Proverbs, or for love – like Psalms, and the Song of Songs.

Inherently, we cannot compare today's writings to those of old. We may also find that we may learn, in essence, what is important from what was actually written.

By consulting the Bible, and in this case the book of Proverbs, I found that we can all benefit from it, and this was the reason for writing this short book.

I only took eight verses, one subject, as it appeared only in this specific chapter, to contemplate here with you – the whole book of Proverbs would, most probably, take a lifetime to contemplate and write upon.

The reason I chose these specific eight verses is in an answer to the tacit questions appearing in the minds of so many people this days, or for that matter in the last almost two hundred years.

When in doubt – go back to basics.

When confusion sets in – look to simplify the conditions, so you may find simpler solution that may lead you to clarity.

Society today seems to think that the fact that we have advanced in technology and machinery, the fact that we can produce food more easily, the fact that we might know more about diseases, justifies our dismissal of wisdom of old.

I have mentioned earlier that it seems that Human nature has not changed, and therefore, our disregard to wisdom of old is entirely unfounded.

Throughout the generations, in all countries, in all religions and belief systems, we find that people yearn for happiness and joy. They look at success, as uplifting while, failure is deemed depressing.

Yes, it is possible and important to learn from failure, but surely, if we have learnt we will cease to fail so many times.

By having Free Will and the power of choice, we should realise that we were given responsibility – that we are not automaton!

Exercising our power of choice should span right from the moment of conceiving an idea, through all the stages it requires to manifest. While on our journey, our attitudes are required to change if we are to accomplish it.

By following the good advice of Solomon the King, we may insure an easier facilitation of it.

Why would wisdom even exist, if it was not for it to be used?

Why wisdom was not to be cherished, if it was not for its ability to ease our lives, and maybe even save them?

Why wisdom was not to be passed on, if it were for the love we feel for our dear ones?

Why should we ignore the wisdom's existence, and re-invent the wheel time, and time again?

Why should we reject gestures of love and care?

I can ask million more questions, but I am sure you understand my viewpoint whereby, you do not have to follow any advice, new or old, but you might just learn something from it, if only you would listen.

This is the reason Solomon the King started these eight verses, by asking you to listen.

Take care, dear reader, take care of your heart, as well as the hearts of those you deal with, lead by example.

May your journey be interesting, but with the lease amount of strife – rather, have joy.

A word about this series

In this busy day and age, where people have more input than they sometimes able to concentrate on, I venture to offer a more succinct manner of dealing with subjects of interest, or need.

The image of a tip of an iceberg immediately brings to mind that there is much more unseen, underwater if you may.

Consciousness is very much like the waters of a vast sea whereby, our conscious thoughts are those that exist above the water level, and our submerged portion of the conscious – is very much our unknown part therefore, many times, it is called the sub-conscious, or the un-conscious.

Our feelings are just the waves, and wave crests, which are created by the winds of time, and occurrences of life upon the surface.

I would like to have your brief time of contemplation in reading this short book yet, to impress your mind with a profound message, and content.

It is in the succinct that we may never be overwhelmed, and in overpowering vast amount of input that we are fatigued.

I trust you know that much more could have been said about the subject of the book, but maybe what was said is enough.

I wish you joy and peace – always.

Notes

Notes

Notes

Notes

Notes

Notes

www.ingramcontent.com/pod-product-compliance
Lightning Source LLC
Chambersburg PA
CBHW020254090426
42735CB00010B/1923